OAMAR

History & Heritage

Gavin McLean

University of Otago Press

Photographs: All photographs are by the author, except where acknowledged.
Maps by Chris Edkins (p. 5) and Allan J. Kynaston (pp. 18, 36, 46).
Printed by Wyatt & Wilson Print Ltd, Christchurch

Acknowledgements
I would like to thank Joan and Murray McLean for introducing me to Oamaru; Rodney Grater, Neil Plunket, Helen Stead and all the others who have preserved it. Bruce McCulloch, Kathleen Stringer, Tom Heyes and Rodney Grater read the text and offered helpful comments. Thanks to the Alexander Turnbull Library, North Otago Museum and Wellington Public Library for photographs and information. Finally, thanks, too, to Elaine Marland and Chris Cochran in Wellington, and in Oamaru to Sally and Des Cochrane at the Anne Mieke Guest House and Michael O'Brien for the whisky and words.

Photographs
Front cover: The Forrester Gallery shines at night.

Back cover, top: The Oamaru breakwater and Holmes Wharf (left, rear) from Grave's Walkway.

Back cover, bottom: Oamaru rocks! The Penguin Café, down an alleyway off Harbour Street, is one of the country's more surreal live music venues.

Page 1: Spot the dummy: Whitestone Civic Trust chairperson Bruce McCulloch (centre rear), Wendy Burke (front) and Gordon Price (right) promote Traditional Boats Day. Despite occasional appearances to the contrary, Oamaru's costumed 'Living Victorians' seldom bite.

*Poster, Totara Estate.
Believe it or not.*

Further Information
Oamaru Visitor Centre, 1 Thames Street,
     ph. (03) 434-1656, fax (03) 434-1657; www.tourism.waitaki.co.nz
Oamaru Whitestone Civic Trust, 2 Harbour Street,
     ph. (03) 434-5385, fax (03) 434-5381, email: owct@xtra.co.nz
North Otago Museum, 60 Thames Street,
     ph. (03) 434-8060, fax (03) 434-1649;
     www.northotagomuseum.co.nz.

Further Visits
See the Visitor Centre for leaflets on the Janet Frame Heritage Trail and the Historic Port Trail, as well as information about tours and personally guided walks.

Contents

1   A Short History of Oamaru *page 7*
Early history *8*; Oamaru's evolution *11*; heritage makes history *14*; Oamaru walks *17*

2   Oamaru Walk 1:
Thames Street/Gardens Walk *page 19*
Lower Thames Street *19*, Oamaru public gardens *30*; Itchen Street *31*

3   Oamaru Walk 2: Historic Precinct Walk *page 37*
Itchen Street *37*; Tyne Street *38*; Harbour Street *42*; Grain Elevator *45*

4   Oamaru Walk 3: Historic Port Walk *page 47*
Wansbeck Street *47*; Port of Oamaru *50*; blue penguin colony *52*; Grave's Walkway *53*

5   Town & Around *page 55*
Old freezing works *55*; railway station *56*; St Patrick's Basilica *57*; Totara Estate *59*; Clark's Flourmill *61*; Parkside Quarry *62*

     Oamaru Events Calendar *page 64*

Tens of thousands of people now visit Oamaru's successful blue penguin colony by the breakwater.

Enjoy Oamaru. Take your time in Tyne Street.

Check out the wetland garden by the grain elevator.

Discover Oamaru's outlying points of interest by following the route in Town and Around (p.55).

Use the map opposite to drive to the Parkside Limestone Quarry (p. 62), Totara Estate (p. 59), and Clark's Flourmill (p. 61).

Another day, take the coastal scenic route through Kakanui and All Day Bay to Waianakarua and return via State Highway 1. Moeraki, Katiki Beach and Trotters Gorge are also good places to visit, to the south, and don't overlook the Waitaki Valley, inland to the north.

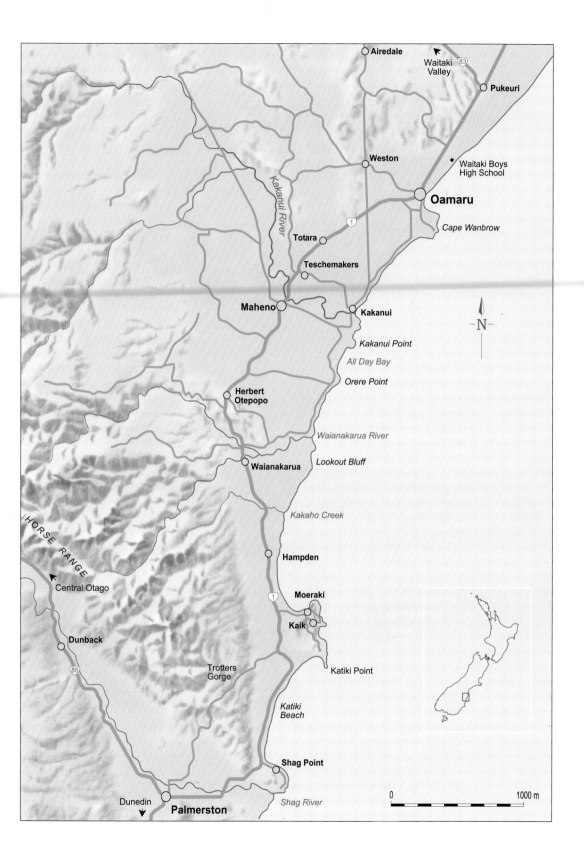

Oamaru developed as an open roadstead. This sort of shipping service was expensive, slow and dangerous, and the town developed a reputation of being one of the colony's most dangerous ports. North Otago Museum

Sir George Grey needed no spin-doctors. In 1878 the old flatterer asked his audience 'what name ought to be given to Oamaru?' then answered, 'well, I said, from her youth I will call her a maiden; she has youth and beauty. Then as I looked at your buildings rising in stone of the utmost brilliance, of a kind I have never seen before, I thought, Oamaru is a fair maiden that sits by the sea'. Locals lapped the compliment up and still trot it out. The limestone that caught Grey's eye has earned Oamaru the label 'Whitestone City'. The 'city' part has always been wishful thinking, but 'Whitestone' lingers today, even on award-winning products not normally associated with durability, such as chicken and cheese.

In the 1980s, architectural historian John Stacpoole described Harbour and Tyne Streets as 'reminiscent of Italy – here if anywhere in New Zealand, Antonio might have bewailed his ship's wreck or Tybalt duelled with Romeo'. Novelist Maurice Shadbolt likened it to a deserted film set: an apt observation, for, like studio props, the elaborate limestone buildings offer a chocolate-box view of only part of Oamaru's history, what Peter Shaw has called the 'Architecture of Prosperity'. In the days when the town enjoyed the sorry distinction of being the best built and most-mortgaged in the colony, its streets held plenty of wooden shacks, tents and dives. Within stumbling distance of the first elegant classical buildings, a vast crater in lower Thames Street lurked in the darkness, awaiting the unwary and the inebriated. Oamaru's streets were paved not with gold but with mud, dust and dung.

When the insightful historian K.C. McDonald studied 1878 Oamaru he described a youthful town, but one with an appalling death rate of twelve per thousand. One baby in twelve failed to survive its first year. It paid to have wealthy, healthy parents here. Nor was the class struggle absent. During the 1890s, Oamaru was the national stronghold of the shearers' bitter struggle against the squatters, represented by Thomas Brydone's New Zealand and Australian Land Company and similar businesses, whose buildings still dot the township.

Victorian Oamaru was anything but quiet. McDonald wrote of 'groups of mere boys, sometimes intoxicated, obstructing the footpaths and shocking the ears of passers-by with obscene language, and crowding peaceful citizens into the gutters'. Larrikins even disrupted church services by banging on windows, shouting or throwing stones. Not that the 'cure' was necessarily better. From September 1883, Salvation Army hit squads pushed their unwelcome way into the bars to proclaim the message of abstinence, obliging some Oamaruvians to declare that they preferred the drunks' slurred philosophising to the Salvationists' raucous preaching, singing and music!

Listen to another historian, Erik Olssen: 'almost all of the hotels remained open until midnight and, despite the law, most of them permitted gambling, dancing and singing. In each year convictions for drunkenness in Oamaru trebled the national figure. Men fought, swore and pissed in public'. Dunedin's *Age* newspaper called Oamaru 'that drunken metropolis'. The unlicensed premises were worse than the regulated dives. Wild orgies spilled out into the streets from scores of unlicensed grog-shops, which masqueraded as boarding houses. Not everyone drank of course, but so many did that in 1881 the *Oamaru Mail*, ineffectively flailing the dead horse of prohibition, raged impotently about the existence of thirty-two sly-grog-shops and twelve brothels, on top of the legal premises.

EARLY HISTORY

How did this all begin? Polynesian settlement of New Zealand began just under 1000 years ago. North Otago's hinterland bears the marks of several centuries of Polynesian/Maori economic activity – from the seasonal rock shelters up the Waitaki Valley, decorated with art, to the moa butcheries and settlements at the mouths of the Shag and Waitaki rivers. East Coast North Island Kai Tahu invaded the mainland in the 18th century but probably made only modest use of Oamaru, preferring Moeraki and the rivers. Oamaru's attraction would be the limited shelter that it gave to the deep-draft oceangoing ships of the next colonisers, the British.

In 1848 the large-scale systematic European settlement of Otago began, and not everyone got a bargain. That year 'Kemp's Purchase' took much of the South Island from Maori for a pittance and pseudo-theocratic Free Church colonists sailed into Otago Harbour to found the new Otago settlement. At first they stuck close to Dunedin, leaving North Otago to the runholders. The European architectural history of Oamaru began modestly in 1853, when runholder Hugh Robison erected a sod hut on the north side of the creek. Five years later H.C. Hertslet arrived from Moeraki to take over the landing service. In 1858, Charles Traill and Henry France opened the first small wooden stores on the beach near the landing site. Others followed and the infant settlement surged ahead from about 1860. Oamaru had 207 inhabitants by 1861 and 730 by 1864, most earning their living by servicing the gold rushes and the pastoralists, whose wool and grain (mainly wheat), built the commercial heart of the historic precinct that you see today.

Oamaru's Name

Scholars continue to ponder the origins of Oamaru's name. No one knows for certain. Either 'Ohamaru' or 'Ohamara' appeared on a European map in 1841 but within a few years Edward Shortland was spelling it 'Oamaru'.

There are four guesses. The lamest attributes it to the Maori for a tree, amaru. More widely accepted is that it derives from the name of a person or mythical figure, Maru. Others suggest that the 'o' may be an obsolete word for food, or offering to a deity, meaning an offering of food to Maru. Finally, it could derive from etymological association with maru, which has shelter as one of its meanings.

© North Otago Museum

North Otago Museum

Foremost of the architects who exploited the qualities of Oamaru Stone was Thomas Forrester (left, photographed in the Oamaru Harbour Board Office with A. G. Creagh). This Glasgow-born plasterer and polymath emigrated to Otago in 1861 and moved to Oamaru eight years later to supervise construction of the Bank of Otago (page 21). Although he spent the rest of his life working for the Oamaru Harbour Board, from 1872 he also practised part-time as an architect until 1890 when his business partner, John Lemon, died. In 2002 the Historic Places Trust published a major assessment of his architecture, Forrester & Lemon of Oamaru: Architects.

The little town's tradesmen included some self-taught architects. From the 1860s they began to work with the local limestone that hotelier Richard Jones had used so successfully in 1861 in a (now neglected) stable behind his Star and Garter hotel. There was no looking back. Oamaru Stone, a creamy white limestone, has many virtues and few vices. It is very pure (over ninety-five per cent calcium carbonate) and as the stone company explains, 'this purity, together with the mild amount of lithification that the deposit has undergone, give it the property of a free-stone'. In other words, you can cut it with a saw. If cut on its natural bed and laid so that it does not absorb salt and moisture, it can be remarkably durable, gaining strength with age. To round out a happy story, Oamaru Stone was plentiful and was cheaper than the timber North Otago lacked. Soon architects such as Dunedin's Robert Lawson and the local Forrester & Lemon were turning out classically inspired and Victorian Italianate structures that oozed civic and commercial pride. As Olssen observed, 'Oamaru's leaders celebrated, in gleaming white limestone, the triumphs of the pioneers and the certainty of progress through capitalism'.

Progress was bumpy rather than certain, almost entirely dependent on the port. The open roadstead quickly developed an evil reputation, claiming around twenty-five shipwrecks in less than twenty years. Early port planning was farcical. In 1868 a storm

wrecked the first jetty, exposed to the elements and three ships. Chagrined, the town resolved to build a dock in the narrow Oamaru Creek, then changed tack and opted for an artificial harbour in the lee of Cape Wanbrow. In 1874, the Oamaru Dock Trust became the Oamaru Harbour Board, which extended the breakwater commenced by the trust. Macandrew Wharf, opened in 1875, virtually ended shipwrecks at the port and nine years later Oamaru had the honour of berthing the first steamer built especially for the frozen meat trade to Britain, the *Elderslie*. Sumpter Wharf confirmed Oamaru as a major export port and the town ended the 1870s as New Zealand's ninth-largest centre. Rail connections to Dunedin and to Christchurch further enhanced its attractiveness.

But the harbour board had over-reached itself. It defaulted on a loan in 1891 and went into receivership three years later. The Long Depression of the 1880s killed Oamaru's remarkable growth spurt. The town's population peaked at 5791 in 1881, then fell and would not reach the 1881 figure for more than forty years. Nevertheless, a little progress continued. During the 1880s woollen mills (1881) and freezing works (1886) were established. Coastal erosion later swept away the first woollen mill, but you can still see the old freezing works just north of the historic precinct. Ironically, refrigeration's success came at the expense of grain, whose warehouses still dominate that precinct.

Wansbeck Street in about 1880. The Emmanuel Congregational Church on the right has not survived, but you can still see the Northern Hotel, the terrace shops and Columba Church on the left. North Otago Museum

© North Otago Museum

A train thunders across the creek early last century. In the background are two buildings which survive, albeit without all their original finery: the massive Grain Elevator (left) and the Connell & Clowes building, now the Woolstore. The latter should remind urban designers and other aesthetic sterilisers that the Victorians and Edwardians loved to use buildings and streets for advertising. North Otago Museum

OAMARU'S EVOLUTION

When you walk around Oamaru you may find a few generalisations helpful. At the risk of over-simplifying, the further north you go, the more recent things are. The first commercial district spread along the west side of Tyne Street in 1860. It rebuilt itself in stone from the mid 1860s, creating the Scottish Society Hall, Easymade Marmalade and Corner Collectables buildings that typify the single-storey general merchants' warehouses of the time. Wansbeck Street had developed as the first specialised retail node (we will see the terrace shops) and Tees Street also attracted shopkeepers.

Commerce spread out on to the eastern side of Tyne Street and into Harbour Street from the mid 1870s, with the Harbour Street buildings generally being the largest (and, with the exception of the Oamaru Harbour Board building, being devoted almost entirely to grain storage). But for all but port warehouses the trend was northwards along Thames Street after completion of the Thames Street bridge and the new southern entry through Itchen Street. The completion of the railway station in Humber Street in 1900 accelerated the northwards drift. This in turn took development pressure off the old commercial sector, which became Shadbolt's deserted film set, providing cheap space for businesses such as grain and skin buyers, stock and station agents and community groups.

Change continues today. Oamaru's newer commercial buildings are down Coquet Street, and motels and fast food outlets are reshaping the northern end of Thames Street. The Harbour/Tyne Street historic area is attracting new uses and tenants, again changing the nature of the precinct, which now combines tourism and retailing with more traditional functions. Two things have not changed. With few exceptions, the town's streets retain their distinctive British river names. And Thames Street remains one of New Zealand's widest. This is because it was laid out (like Invercargill and Penang) by surveyor J.T. Thompson, who believed that a street should be wide enough to enable a bullock team to turn comfortably. Later generations of teenagers would bless him for designing a street that permitted large old carloads of them to drink under the trees while watching the world cruise by. Before then, Thames Street's muddy, dusty width had been something of an embarrassment. The trees that give central Oamaru character today owe their presence to persistent lobbying by the Beautifying Society (formed in 1908), which dismissed shopkeepers' fears of their obscuring shop signs and (tongue-in-cheek) the claims of the wags who argued that they would hinder the efforts of police in arresting drunks by giving them something to which to cling! The first American elms (since replaced) were planted in the business section of Thames Street in 1914.

Opposite: Oamaru Harbour, probably in April 1932. An overseas freighter is loading at Holmes Wharf while another big 'Home boat' in Shaw Savill colours and a Union Company freighter lie off the breakwater. HMS Wakakura *and a dredge are at Sumpter Wharf.*
North Otago Museum

All these buildings survive, as you will see when you walk down Harbour Street: Connell & Clowes, now the Woolstore (left) and the Criterion (right) frame our view down Harbour Street to the Oamaru Harbour Board offices and A.H. Maude's store (soon to become the Lane's Emulsion building).
North Otago Museum

© North Otago Museum

Since the port's closure to commercial shipping trawlers such as the 91-ton San Bernadette *have been its biggest users.*

The 'Home boats', the big UK-trade refrigerated liners, never returned to Oamaru after the Second World War, but in all other respects the town boomed. Old industries expanded and new ones, confectionery manufacturing and engineering, set up. So, too, did hydroelectric construction up the Waitaki Valley. De Geest's innovative house factory boomed on the back of dam construction and North Otago residents got used to seeing complete houses being trucked up to the new construction villages. Education, already important to Oamaru, expanded further, with secondary schools peaking at five. Population soared from 7481 in 1945 to 12,429 in 1961 and would top 14,000 a decade later. In the early 1970s, though, that spurt fizzled out and then reversed. The port saw its last ship in 1974 and scheduled air services finished just over a decade later. Main trunk passenger rail services ceased in 2002. By way of minor compensation, the sale and public consumption of alcohol became legal again in 1962, signalling the end of trips across the electorate boundaries to Georgetown or Glenavy. The licensing trust did a reasonable job of reopening the old Queens Hotel as the Brydone but condemned its customers to choosing between a grotty tavern in Thames Street and a hideous multi-unit booze barn and car park at the North End.

For a while Oamaru's woollen milling and meat freezing companies prospered. Alliance Textiles and Waitaki Industries took over many competitors but each lost the internal boardroom battles and the head offices left Oamaru. That, plus late 1980s public sector retrenchment and agricultural, banking and financial services restructuring stripped valuable managerial and white-collar jobs from the town. Local government reform in 1989 cut more jobs. In one of the worst performances for a mid-size servicing centre, Oamaru's population tumbled to 12,303 by 1986 and 12,015 in 2001, low-waged and ageing. Proposals in the early 1980s to enlarge and reopen the port to serve planned cement works at Weston never led anywhere. Several Catholic schools closed, although secondary schooling remains important. Elective day surgery ceased in the mid 1990s and the hospital was replaced, controversially, by a much smaller unit on Takaro Park. Oamaru's bedrock real estate prices made embarrassing news, although locals capitalised on it by imaginatively marketing North Otago to Aucklanders keen on buying dirt-cheap dirt. As the 21st century dawned, however, dairy farm conversions, large-scale Japanese investment in organic foods, viticulture and irrigation/electricity developments up the Waitaki Valley, and continuing tourism growth held the prospect of a brighter future.

Events in Oamaru
Many heritage and other events are held in Oamaru during the year. A calendar of these appears on page 64.

Below: Queen Victoria rests between Heritage Weeks in Smith's Grain Store.

HERITAGE MAKES HISTORY

Back in the late 1980s, left dateless and desperate by the new economy, Oamaru decided to tart up its old finery. Locals had already marked many buildings and appreciation of the value of the town's Victorian architecture had been growing from the 1960s, helped by numerous Historic Places Trust classifications from the 1980s. The Trust also bought two historic properties just outside Oamaru, Totara Estate and Clark's Flourmill, but the most important acquisition was probably its 1980 purchase of the old Customs House for conservation and resale. 'Adaptive reuse' had arrived and just in time. As recently as the 1970s, three of the town's oldest buildings – Eustace Roxby's distinctive hip-roofed kauri home (1860) in Tyne Street, the old 1865 former Bank of New Zealand in Tyne Street and the 1860s Pioneer Gallery in Thames Street – had been demolished, the first two for particularly hideous blights on the landscape, a scrapyard and the world's ugliest squash court entrance. A turning point came, however, when the council adapted the Athenaeum and the Bank of New South Wales for cultural purposes (a museum and art gallery respectively). This showed that buildings could take on new lives without unduly compromising their heritage value.

More was to come. In 1988 the Arthur Young feasibility study commissioned by the council recommended forming a civic trust and incrementally imposing a 'Victorian Town at Work' theme on the Harbour/Tyne Street historic precinct. Its suggestion of diverting the main road through Itchen Street was not implemented, but the other main recommendations were. In 1989, with the help of the Alexander McMillan Trust, the new Oamaru Whitestone Civic Trust bought eight buildings in the Harbour/Tyne Street area. It later bought more, most notably in 2001 the deteriorating railway station, ineptly privatised in the 1990s. The Civic Trust has successfully used the theme of a 'Victorian Town at Work' (minus, of course, Victorian Oamaru's larrikins, drunkenness, violence and prolonged depression) to promote the precinct, which now attracts ever more visitors. The November 'Heritage Week' celebrations, with their pith-helmeted, penny-farthing pedalling 'Living Victorians' and outsize Queen Victoria, grow every year, and in March there is also a traditional boats day at the port. An organic

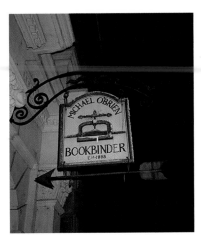 

The historic precinct now houses a range of activities and heritage crafts such as bookbinding (left) and retailing, as well as special events such as 'All-British Day' (right).

food festival highlights the district's efforts to lead the New Zealand organic horticultural industry and thousands now view blue penguins down by the breakwater.

It has not all been plain sailing. Some of the less imaginative still label heritage 'anti-progress' and there has been some confusion about the roles of the local authority, its development board, building owners and heritage advocates. In 1992 the 'Red Lion' flourmill burned down behind Harbour Street. A few years later the council inflicted modern bulbous kerbing on part of the precinct, before protests stopped it. Clumsy engineering and ad hoc development at the historic waterfront ignores its status as an archaeological site and a priceless cultural landscape in its own right. But the setbacks have been comparatively minor. By 2002 the Civic Trust, supported by Lottery funding and community grants, had put sprinkler protection into nearly all of its buildings, had re-roofed most and was conserving them as funding permitted. A conservation plan will address Harbour Street's surface and may yet spare it the concrete fake 'cobblestones' that blight so many Main Street and heritage precincts elsewhere. The example set by this trust and the Historic Places Trust has also encouraged more private owners to treat their buildings with increasing respect. Demolitions have almost stopped and there have been none of the replicas or building relocations that would undermine the town's remarkable authenticity. As a result of this public enterprise and community endeavour, Oamaru entered the 21st century increasingly dependent on its internationally significant 19th century colonial landscape.

What sort of landscape are we talking about? Peter Shaw and Conal McCarthy have written eloquently about the Greek Revival neo-classical and Renaissance influence that Edinburgh would have exercised on architects Robert Lawson, James Johnston and Thomas Forrester. They consciously strove to give a mushrooming colonial whippersnapper the sense of permanence of an established European city many times its size, even if their ostentation frequently stretched no further than the facade. Erik Olssen describes this world of impressive white-stone buildings, 'the grandeur of their facades disguising the shallowness of their depth'. He has a point, as you will see when you enter some of these boxy little structures, or walk around the rear of Tyne Street. But there are other, less aesthetically driven ways of reading this landscape. It is also an intriguing example of the late Victorian 'stratification and Gothicization of the dominions', as David Cannadine has observed. From Toronto to Wellington gentlemen's clubs, grand hotels, railway stations, public schools and cathedrals proliferated as the Empire neared its peak. As we shall see at Waitaki Boys' High School, Oamaru, although slipping behind northern centres, was not immune to this. As the war memorials and the Hall of Memories will also show, it was not protected from the awful consequences, with hundreds of young North Otago men fighting Northern Hemisphere battles.

Oamaru has less of the Scottish Baronial or Gothic Revival styles than other New Zealand centres, but the Classical and Renaissance styles were imperial, and furthermore they stretched further back in time than others. Small it may be compared to 'Marvellous Melbourne', but Oamaru is an expression of pure settler capitalism, the architecture of prosperity and imperialism set in stone. And how quickly it was achieved! Most of what you will see went from quarry to street in a single generation, from Charles Traill and Henry France's wooden stores of 1858 to the collapse of the building boom in 1884. But it is important to remember that the buildings are not necessarily the most important elements in the landscape. The town's prosperity rested on the port and the construction of Holmes Wharf and the shipping basin is undoubtedly Thomas Forrester's most important legacy to Oamaru. Streets and bridges were almost as important, for as we shall see, the Itchen Street cutting and the Thames Street bridge were second only to the port in creating (and, ironically, preserving) what you are about to enjoy.

John Megget Forrester (1865–1965) took over his father's architectural practice in 1890 and, as we shall see on our walks, he also designed many fine buildings. He retired in 1931, turning his practice over to Ivan Steenson, who had joined him eleven years earlier. Mayor of Oamaru from 1931 to 1933, Forrester kept himself busy during his long retirement by serving on many social and cultural groups. North Otago Museum

OAMARU WALKS

Three of the walks described here cover most of Oamaru's historical, architectural and natural highlights. Walk 1, the Thames Street/Gardens Walk, and Walk 2, the Historic Precinct Walk, start and finish at the Visitor Centre in lower Thames Street. Walk 1 features the commercial and public buildings and places that flourished after the creek was bridged and commerce started to drift north. The Historic Precinct Walk takes you around the old commercial heart of Oamaru, built between the early 1860s and the mid 1880s to service the port. Walk 3, the Historic Port Walk, is a longer, more varied trek, taking you around the port, the town's very beginnings, out to two of its 20th century natural heritage initiatives, Grave's Walkway and the penguin colony. Feel free to mix and match elements from these walks as time, interest or weather permits. Penguin colony visitors, for example, might like to take in the Tyne Street buildings on their way down to the breakwater.

There are too many buildings to feature in depth in the text. I have mentioned the significant ones not given individual entries at least briefly in passing. For featured places, the name, location and Historic Places Trust registration category leads the entry. Category I indicates 'places of special or outstanding historical or cultural heritage significance or value'. Category II are 'places of historical or cultural heritage significance or value'. As you will see, Oamaru is extraordinarily richly endowed with examples of both Category I and II places.

On Sundays and public holidays the Oamaru Steam and Rail Restoration Society's 1924 steam train runs from the 'Harbourside' station behind the Visitor Centre to the Red Sheds at the port, carboniferously filling the precinct with the stench of good old Victorian smoke.

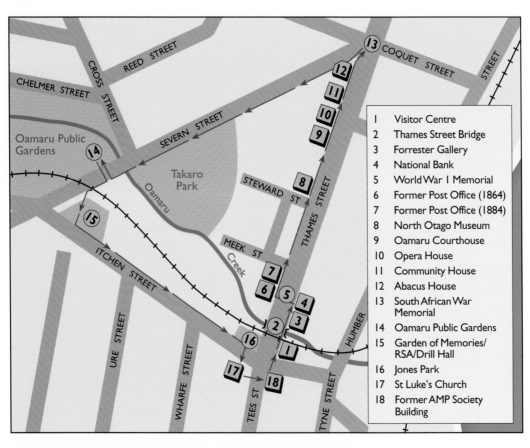

CROSS STREET
REED STREET
CHELMER STREET
SEVERN STREET
Oamaru Public Gardens
Takaro Park
Oamaru Creek
STEWARD ST
MEEK ST
ITCHEN STREET
URE STREET
WHARFE STREET
TEES ST
TYNE STREET
HUMBER
THAMES STREET
COQUET STREET
STREET

14
15
13
12
11
10
9
8
7
6
5
4
3
2
1
16
17
18

1	Visitor Centre
2	Thames Street Bridge
3	Forrester Gallery
4	National Bank
5	World War 1 Memorial
6	Former Post Office (1864)
7	Former Post Office (1884)
8	North Otago Museum
9	Oamaru Courthouse
10	Opera House
11	Community House
12	Abacus House
13	South African War Memorial
14	Oamaru Public Gardens
15	Garden of Memories/ RSA/Drill Hall
16	Jones Park
17	St Luke's Church
18	Former AMP Society Building

1. Visitor Centre
Start your visit here at the bottom of Thames Street. The tourist train runs to the port from the tiny 'Harbourside' station to the left.

1. VISITOR CENTRE (former Colonial Bank)

1 Thames Street (HPT II)

Although this building housed the Oamaru branch of the Bank of New Zealand from 1895 to 1969, it dates from 1878. Forrester & Lemon designed it for the Colonial Bank, a competitor to the BNZ until the banking crisis of the 1890s, when the government forced through a controversial shotgun wedding between the teetering BNZ, and the terminally ill Colonial. In Oamaru, BNZ staff happily vacated their older Tyne Street premises to move here. After providing a home for the Oamaru Operatic Society, the former Colonial regained its decorative roofline features and became the Visitor Centre. There is a booking office, public toilets and, tucked away to the left of the building, the 'Harbourside' tourist train station.

☞☞ *Walk a few metres north along Thames Street to the bridge.*

2. THAMES STREET BRIDGE

Thames Street (HPT II)

We take bridges for granted but our forebears, who teetered across the Oamaru creek on planks or forded it at the head of the loop in Steward Street before it had been straightened and tamed, certainly did not. Imagine their delight when contractors began a handsome six-metre wide, stone bridge late in 1860. Nine years later it gained footpaths and iron railings and later still spread out to the full width of the street. By then the council had completed the Itchen Street cutting that linked lower Thames Street to the town's Severn Street southern entrance. Retailing's northwards march up Thames Street commenced, to the detriment of Wansbeck Street. As we shall see, people would still build in Harbour, Tyne and Tees streets, but their backwater status was looming.

In fair weather you can walk under the bridge along a track that starts behind the Visitor Centre and comes out the other side, via stepping-stones, between the toilets and the old post office. Look up to see where the bridge was widened in stages. But for this walk come back to this side of Thames Street. Two Oamaru icons, the former Banks of Otago and New South Wales, await.

☞☞ *Walk to the Forrester Gallery.*

2. Thames Street Bridge
The Visitor Centre peers over the Thames Street Bridge. The creek was no Amazon but its natural course twisted more than a campaigning colonial politician and it greatly inconvenienced early Oamaruvians.

3. Forrester Gallery
The Oamaru Borough Council
strengthened the old bank and
reopened it in 1983 as the
Forrester Gallery.

3. FORRESTER GALLERY
(former Bank of New South Wales)
9 Thames Street (HPT I)

This is a case of portico envy if ever there was one. A decade
after the Bank of Otago built Robert Lawson's beautiful classical
bank, the Bank of New South Wales commissioned him to go one
better. While the 1883 building is larger, it does not overshadow
its 1873 neighbour. Lawson kept within the familiar classical
vocabulary, increasing the Corinthian columns from four to six
and replacing the triangular pediment with an elaborate
balustrade. That balustrade has lost some of its detailing but the
interior has weathered changing fashions better; the elaborate
plaster ceiling from the old banking chamber is striking. Since
1983 the Forrester Gallery (named after the architect, John Megget
Forrester, whose legacy helped to establish the art gallery) has
made the temple of commerce a temple of art and learning.

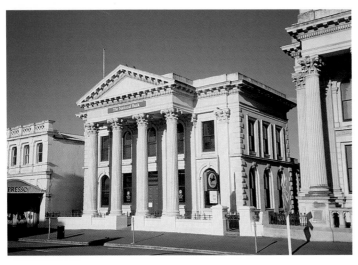

4. National Bank
Framed by the Empire Hotel
(left) and the Forrester Gallery
(right), the National Bank
building has been an Oamaru
landmark for 130 years.

4. NATIONAL BANK (former Bank of Otago)

11 Thames St (HPT I)

The British-owned Bank of Otago opened a branch in rented premises in Oamaru in 1866. Five years later it stamped its mark on the town with this limestone leviathan, which 'with its pillared portico, would have been an ornament to any town in the country, even if it did look like a temple strayed from Athens'. Strayed or not, the temple had better staying power than the Bank of Otago. In 1873 another British-owned bank, the National Bank, moved in, never to shift. Some of its staff matched its staying power. Willoughby McDouall, inherited in the 1873 takeover, managed the Oamaru branch from 1882 until 1914, kept here because his superiors thought him too valuable a local institution to move on. Scottish-trained architect Robert Lawson, who had left Melbourne to design Dunedin's First Church, turned to the Italian Renaissance palazzo style favoured by commercial premises in his native Edinburgh. Carver Louis Godfrey produced the elaborate capitals on the columns.

☞ ☞ *Beside the bank is the Empire Hotel (1867). However we will now cross Thames Street, stopping to inspect the war memorial on the traffic island.*

*5. World War I Memorial
The Empire Hotel (left) and National Bank (right) form up behind the War Memorial.*

5. WORLD WAR I MEMORIAL (1926)

Thames Street (HPT II)

The 19th century crashed to ruins in the horrors of the First World War. The South African War Memorial (page 29) speaks of imperial pride and triumph. Not this one. On a base of Bluff granite, T.J. Clapperton's bronze soldier consoles a small child against a 13-metre high tapering column of Sicilian granite. The child symbolises the ideals of humanity for which the war was meant to have been waged.

North Otago people just about went to war over the memorial itself. They argued for months about whether it should be utilitarian or inspirational. Then they argued about whether it should bear the names of the dead. After deciding against that, they fought about where to put it. Finally they chose E. Miller's design. Viscount Jellicoe laid the foundation stone on 14 October 1924. On Anzac Day 1926 Lieut.-Colonel J. Hargest unveiled the memorial and placed in a locked receptacle a bronze casket containing the names of the district's soldiers who had served overseas.

☞ ☞ *Cross Thames Street and stop outside the smaller former post office.*

6. & 7. FORMER POST OFFICES

20 & 12 Thames Street (HPT I (1864), II (1884))

Only Oamaru has two masonry post offices side-by-side. Colonial Architect William Clayton's little Italianate building (1864), is dwarfed by the post office completed just twenty years later. In fact it has suffered at its successor's expense, because a northern wing added in 1869 to house the Customs Department came down to make room for the 1884 building, leaving this one looking a little short-changed and lop-sided. To add insult to injury, the clock planned for the tower was never installed. Clayton's building later housed the Social Welfare Department, amongst others, but now caters for better-heeled clients.

Forrester & Lemon's large 1884 building started with neither clock nor the elaborate tower they had designed for it. Blame a classic central government/local government spat, with Wellington refusing to build the tower until the borough council paid for a clock. The council refused, so the building sat squat and silly until 1894 when the government relented and put up the tower. The clock and chimes took longer (1903) and were the gift of pastoralist St. John McLean Buckley (whose 'Redcastle' mansion forms the heart of St Kevin's College at the north end of town). Thomas Forrester had retired by then, so his son John Megget Forrester did the job. John's simple, French-influenced mansard-roofed tower sits slightly oddly; his father had planned an ornate cupola-topped structure.

Post office restructuring in the late 1980s left this building empty. Fortunately conservationists persuaded the new district council to move in here instead of building a new gin palace elsewhere. There is a post-box by the War Memorial but Oamaruvians wanting to make fuller use of the postal service now use a former service station and store.

☞ ☞ Continue north to the museum. Steward Street, which leads down to Takaro Park and the swimming pool, contains interesting old buildings, the bridge club and the 1892 Royal Foundation for the Blind premises.

8. NORTH OTAGO MUSEUM

Corner Thames and Steward Streets (HPT II)

The Victorian middle class preached the secular gospel of self-improvement and peppered colonial towns with lodges, friendly societies and other institutions. Mechanics' institutes, an idea imported from Britain, strove to educate and 'improve' workers through access to books and lectures. The grandly named Oamaru Athenaeum and Mechanics' Institute emerged in 1865 under decidedly middle-class leadership. Despite seesawing interest/ apathy, it erected a plain stone building on this site in 1867 and the next year appointed George Orr librarian. The middle class made better use of the place than the mechanics it purported to serve. After the *North Otago Times* slammed the old building as 'more like a dead-house or a neglected boat-shed than a public institution', the Institute asked committee member Thomas Forrester to design this one. He produced the sort of neo-classical design that was almost de rigueur for buildings of this type, picking up classical references to Athene, goddess of arts and crafts in the detached Ionic (lower) and Corinthian (upper) columns supporting the detached triangular pediment. In 1948 the council turned the Athenaeum into the municipal library. Here Janet Frame's old men sat 'petrified by the silence notices'. After the present library opened on the adjacent Pioneer Gallery site in 1975, the Athenaeum became the North Otago Museum.

8. North Otago Museum Although Oamaruvians collected and displayed artefacts in the 19th century, the museum's real precursor was the North Otago Pioneer Gallery, opened by George Meek in the old courthouse in 1953. Twenty years later the Oamaru Borough Council took it over and appointed a full-time director. The revitalised North Otago Museum opened in the refurbished Athenaeum on 16 December 1977. Its displays feature natural, Maori and colonial history and it also houses the district archives.

9. Courthouse
(described next page)
The exterior of the Courthouse
is almost unchanged since it
opened in 1883, the major
alteration being the removal of
the chimneys during re-roofing
in the late 1970s.

☞ ☞ Continue north along Thames Street. Just past the library is de
Lamberts (top left), built in the 1920s on the old gaol site to house the de
Lambert brothers' tea importing business. A bit further along, reached
through the alleyway between the legal offices and the shop at 80 Thames
Street is the ruined stables building of the old (1869) gaol (top right). The
gaol sported a hexagonal tower and crenellated parapets that struck K.C.
McDonald as looking 'like the castle of a minor baron'. It closed in 1913,
the year Oamaru lost its Resident Magistrate, and was later demolished.
Just before you reach the courthouse, you will pass more early 20th century
commercial buildings.

9. OAMARU COURTHOUSE (see previous page)

Thames Street (HPT I)

Modern Oamaru is a quiet place but the youthful, male-dominated colonial town could be noisy, violent and drunken. Here, Erik Olssen noted, 'satanic forces ran amok', or at least in the eyes of newspaper proprietor George Jones who, as we have seen, complained in 1881 about fewer than 6000 people keeping twenty hotels, two breweries, thirty-two illegal sly-grog shops and twelve brothels busy. Jones may have had a point, for Oamaru was Otago's roughest town: 'in each year convictions for drunkenness in Oamaru trebled the national figure'.

The first courthouse (1863) ended its days as the Pioneer Gallery (on the site of the present library). Oamaruvians kept it busy, but caseloads gradually reduced, thanks to an ageing population and from the 1880s 'petticoat rule' in the form of the temperance movement. This courthouse, completed in 1883, is generally considered Forrester & Lemon's masterpiece. Unlike its earliest 'clients', its centrally placed temple-front portico with Corinthian columns presents a dignified and sober face to Thames Street. The Supreme Court also sat here until 1931.

☞ ☞ *Walk next door.*

10. OPERA HOUSE

96 Thames Street (HPT I)

Oamaru became a borough in 1866. At first councillors gave higher priority to roads and bridges than to erecting monuments to their own pretensions. They met in the first courthouse, then graced the police's former Itchen Street corner site with a wooden borough chambers that even the borough historian considered 'rather unsightly'. The struggle to build the water supply and keep up with demands for road improvements kept them there while the harbour board and the county council built in style. By the early 1900s, however, businessmen felt that civic pride demanded something better. They called for a combination municipal office and opera house to replace the Theatre Royal, the town's only large public meeting place. Central government gave the land and a loan, but borough and business feuded over building size. Unlike our allegedly enlightened times, business had grander ideas than the politicians. Lawyer Albert Grave (brother of the fund-raising and track-building William George Grave) and Ernest Lee led a group that demanded a second storey, guaranteeing to take long-term leases over the spaces on the upper floor not required by the council. The 765-seat Opera House opened on 7 October 1907, when the mayors of Timaru, Waimate, Dunedin and Invercargill were entertained to a concert. In recent decades the shows put on

10. Opera House
In Owls Do Cry Janet Frame described the unrestrained enthusiasm with which the locals cheered and jeered actors in the second-rate westerns screened by the Opera House, 'the Bughouse'. You can still catch the flicks here.

here have been more 'Oprah' than opera. For many years the Opera House competed with the posher Majestic in Severn St until television killed off movies here. But the circle has turned again and Hollywood's offerings now show at the Opera House, while Pentecostals pray in the Majestic.

☞ ☞ Keep on this side of Thames Street but look through the trees across the intersection to see the old Queen's Hotel, now the Quality Brydone Hotel. It once boasted an elaborate balustrade the equal of any of the buildings we shall see in the historic precinct. Walk next door.

11. COMMUNITY HOUSE
(former Waitaki County Council Offices)
100 Thames Street (HPT II)

County councils administered rural areas after the provincial era ended in 1876. Pastoralist John Campbell chaired the new Waitaki County Council and spent more cautiously than either the harbour board or the borough. James Johnston's handsome building, with its Venetian Renaissance palazzo references, was one of its few early extravagances. In fact, county councillors and staff had to move out six years later to help out the Waitaki Girls' High School, whose premises had been destroyed by fire. The school, very much the poor relative of the boys' high, would squat on this cramped, cheerless site until 1904, when the county moved back in. It remained here until the 1989 local government reforms merged county and borough into the Waitaki District Council.

11. Community House.

☞ ☞ Walk to the next building.

12. *Abacus House*
Abacus House's brickwork contrasts pleasingly with its Oamaru Stone detailing.

12. ABACUS HOUSE

Thames Street (not registered)

Oamaru has many fine brick houses, but fewer brick commercial structures. Abacus House was built in 1919 on the triangular portion of the county council's section. Its original owner, Dalgety & Company, had been trading in Oamaru under various guises almost from the town's beginning. Pastoral firms such as Dalgety underpinned North Otago's economy, advancing farmers money against their harvests, selling farm and station supplies, storing and cleaning grain and wool, and sometimes acting as shipping agents. We shall encounter several former Dalgety buildings in the historic precinct.

☞ ☞ *Walk to the intersection of Thames and Severn Streets and cross to the traffic island, to the South African War Memorial. On the other side of Thames Street you will see several older shops. The 'Polytechnic', with large second-storey windows, was a 'ready-money draper', not a tertiary institution.*

13. South African War Memorial. Although traffic flows have changed, the trooper and the imperial lion on 'The Monument' have not. It looks particularly striking when floodlit at night.

13. SOUTH AFRICAN WAR MEMORIAL

Thames/Severn Streets intersection (HPT II)

Last century Oamaruvians called 'The Monument' the 'Boer War Memorial', but its original name, 'The South African Trooper's Memorial', is closer to modern preferences. War memories were still strong on 2 February 1905 when Lord Plunket unveiled Carlo Bergamini's statue. Many young North Otago men had served in the New Zealand contingents and a lot of grain and feed had been shipped direct from the Oamaru Harbour. No wonder they celebrated imperial supremacy from as far away as North Otago. Italian sculptor Carlo Bergamini based the soldier on local man, David Mickle Jack, but the monument is a polyglot assortment of materials. The concrete foundation and Port Chalmers bluestone base are local, but the rest comes from Victoria (the dressed Malmesbury stone plinth) and Europe (granite and marble). Solicitor, climber and explorer William G. Grave raised most of the £1700 by cycling around the district, extracting donations from virtually every household and charging just five shillings for expenses!

☞ ☞ *Return to the intersection, then walk south along the eastern edge of Severn Street, flanked on our right by the avenue of trees commemorating a past mayor of Oamaru, Dr K. McAdam. On our left are two art deco delights, public toilets worthy of Flash Gordon (above) and the 1940 Centennial Plunket Rooms and Early Settlers' Hall. Across the road are the former Majestic Theatre, the 1889 Baptist Church and the 1919 Police Station. Keep to this side of the street, skirting the edge of Takaro Park, where the new hospital incorporates the old Middle School (HPT II), controversially included in the development of the town's new mini hospital.*

There are two ways of crossing Severn Street to the Oamaru Public Gardens. If mud turns you on, use the walkway under the bridge over the creek; or, cross carefully at street level and go through the main gates.

Middle School (1876).

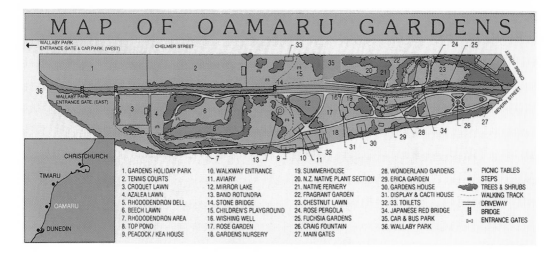

1. GARDENS HOLIDAY PARK	10. WALKWAY ENTRANCE	19. SUMMERHOUSE	28. WONDERLAND GARDENS	⧆ PICNIC TABLES
2. TENNIS COURTS	11. AVIARY	20. N.Z. NATIVE PLANT SECTION	29. ERICA GARDEN	≡ STEPS
3. CROQUET LAWN	12. MIRROR LAKE	21. NATIVE FERNERY	30. GARDENS HOUSE	TREES & SHRUBS
4. AZALEA LAWN	13. BAND ROTUNDRA	22. FRAGRANT GARDEN	31. DISPLAY & CACTI HOUSE	WALKING TRACK
5. RHODODENDRON DELL	14. STONE BRIDGE	23. CHESTNUT LAWN	32. 33. TOILETS	DRIVEWAY
6. BEECH LAWN	15. CHILDREN'S PLAYGROUND	24. ROSE PERGOLA	34. JAPANESE RED BRIDGE	BRIDGE
7. RHODODENDRON AREA	16. WISHING WELL	25. FUCHSIA GARDENS	35. CAR & BUS PARK	⋈ ENTRANCE GATES
8. TOP POND	17. ROSE GARDEN	26. CRAIG FOUNTAIN	36. WALLABY PARK	
9. PEACOCK / KEA HOUSE	18. GARDENS NURSERY	27. MAIN GATES		

14. OAMARU PUBLIC GARDENS

Severn and Chelmer Streets (HPT several items registered)

Map courtesy of Waitaki District Council

The Oamaru Public Gardens are some of the country's finest. Here Oamaru welcomed distinguished visitors such as governors and governors-general, the Duke of Gloucester in 1935 and Queen Elizabeth II and Prince Philip in 1974. In 1865 the provincial government set aside 13.8 hectares for a 'reserve for public gardens' in a swampy area between Chelmer and Isis streets, but the new borough council, preferring what is now King George Park, laid out the first reserve halfway up Tyne Street. In 1876, however, it discovered the well-hidden charms of the Chelmer Street reserve; for all its swampiness and scruffiness, it was larger and more sheltered than Tyne Street. Borough gardener James Kidd straightened the creek, created lakelets and planted assiduously. The Waitaki Acclimatisation Society and the Oamaru Beautifying Society also helped.

There is much to see and to delight the senses. The ornate Severn Street gates come from John Reid's Elderslie estate. Inside there is another Reid gift, the old Elderslie Gazebo, relocated here in 1947. Other highlights include the Carrara marble Craig Fountain (1915), just inside the main entrance and the band rotunda (1915). Pride of place, though, goes to the Wonderland Statue (1926, HPT I). London sculptor Thomas J. Clapperton created its bronze boy and girl peering into fairyland for donor Robert Milligan, a former mayor, harbour board and power board chairman. Nearby is a striking Japanese red bridge (1928), part of a distinctive oriental garden.

14. Oamaru Public Gardens
The Japanese red bridge (1928) is a highlight of the gardens.

☞ ☞ *Once you have seen the gardens cross Severn Street to enter the small memorial gardens. Before you cross, you will see Severn Street's distinctive stone walling (HPT II) running up the hill. The trees are a First World War memorial.*

15. Garden of Memories
The Garden of Memories
provides a pleasant place for
reflection.

15. GARDEN OF MEMORIES AND RSA ROOMS/DRILL HALL

Corner Severn and Itchen Streets (not registered)

The Severn Street end of Itchen Street has a distinctive military precinct, the Garden of Memories, RSA complex and the Volunteer Drill Hall. We have seen Oamaru's other war memorials in Thames Street. The Garden of Memories commemorates the Second World War and later conflicts. Quiet and possessing none of the heroic military iconography of the Thames Street statues, the garden was approved, K.C. McDonald said judiciously, 'after some, but by no means excessive controversy'. The adjacent RSA clubrooms (1950) and bowling green were also part of the project. Next we come to the Volunteer Hall, or 'the Drill Hall' as it is better known, its plain façade relieved by a hint of crenellation. Oamaru formed its first Volunteer unit in 1865, the first of several that enjoyed fluctuating support in the decades to come. The hall was built in 1906, much of the money being raised by women. It once also showed silent movies.

15. Looking out over its
handsome greens, the RSA
building sits between the
Garden of Memories and the
Drill Hall.

☞ ☞ *Walk east along Itchen Street, gateway to the 'new' Oamaru of the 1860s. In the gully is the former J. & T. Meek flourmill (HPT II), once Australasia's largest. After passing a carpet warehouse, for long the fire station, you will reach Jones Park on the corner of Itchen and Thames streets.*

The former J. & T. Meek flourmill (HPT II).

16. JONES PARK

Corner Itchen and Thames Streets (not registered)

We have the Beautifying Society to thank for preventing this, the site of the old borough council chambers, from becoming a coal-yard. Instead it created a garden and memorial arch to George Jones, who had died two years earlier. Who was George Jones? Well, he was important enough for Chief Justice Sir Robert Stout and Managing Director of the *Otago Daily Times*, Sir George Fenwick, to turn up at the unveiling in 1922.

Jones was born at Lower Hutt in 1844 to a violin-playing Wesleyan bootmaker and his wife. George inherited his father's interest in music and later successfully conducted the Oamaru Garrison Band for over a decade. But if a tune was seldom absent from his lips, it was printer's ink that flowed through his veins. In 1877 he took over the struggling, young *Evening Mail* (renamed the *Oamaru Mail* in 1879). It might have sunk had its new proprietor not provided the paper with some of its best copy. In 1877 Parliament hauled him before its privileges committee for describing a Native Land Bill as 'A Bill to further Enrich, at the Expense of the Colony, the Attorney-General and his Colleagues in Land Speculations'. Imprisoned for refusing to apologise, he developed a wide following when he was tried and acquitted on a charge of criminal libel next year. *The Evening Mail*'s circulation doubled. Jones kept making headlines. This outspoken crusader for prohibition and female suffrage entered Parliament in 1880 just to defeat the squattocracy personified by John Reid of Elderslie. In 1895 he entered the old upper house, the Legislative Council, one of the controversial nominations that the Colonial Office had to chastise Governor Glasgow for trying to block. In 1908 Jones bought the *Southland Daily News*, with two sons running the *Mail* and another the *News*.

☞ ☞ Jones Park faces the Visitor Centre but before finishing there we have two more stops to make. Cross to the church on your right.

16. Jones Park
Jones Park offers a pleasant place to relax as well as fine views of St Luke's and the lower Thames Street buildings.

17. St Luke's Church
(opposite, description next page)
This superbly sited church is a fine example of Gothic Revival architecture.

17. ST LUKE'S CHURCH
Corner Itchen and Tees streets (HPT I)

St Luke's elevated corner site, stone walls and mature trees and shrubs make this soaring Gothic Revival whitestone triumph one of Oamaru's most beautiful places. Like St. Patrick's Basilica (page 57), however, it was a long time a-building. Anglican services began in January 1862 and the first permanent minister, the Rev. Algernon Gifford, covered a parish that stretched from Moeraki to the Waitaki River and inland as far as Ohau. Construction of Edward Rumsey and George Jackson's church began in 1865 and the first stage, the southern end of the nave, was consecrated in 1866. It soon proved inadequate, so the nave was completed to its full length in 1876, although the chancel at the end had to be a temporary wooden one. The distinctive 38.7-metre high spire and chancel did not appear until 1913. Richard Greenaway records that John Delacourt Russell, 'a vigorous minister of "endearing eccentricities" climbed the scaffolding and held a cross in position at the top of the spire while artisans fixed it into the stonework'. John Megget Forrester designed the spire and chancel, along with the west porch in 1922. Much of the wood in the chancel is Southland beech and most of the building's woodcarving was the work of English-trained church carver F.G. Gurnsey. Pamphlets and historic photographs tell the story of the building.

There is more to this site than the church. The adjacent John Megget Forrester-designed vicarage (1912) and parish hall (1897) form an attractive miniature religious precinct, rising above stone walling (1901 but replaced 1989–93). Important trees include Norfolk pines, planted in 1878 to commemorate Bishop Selwyn and Bishop Patterson.

☞ ☞ Either explore Tees Street or cross it to the former AMP Building.

17. The St Luke's vicarage and church hall complete the church grounds.

Tees Street's shops suffered as the commercial district drifted north but it is worth exploring if you have a few minutes. It, too, is remarkably authentic. The small shop closest to St Luke's carries a plaque honouring the birth of Lanes Emulsion, whose factory we shall see soon (p. 43). Further along the street is the narrow little former Theosophical Society building (right).

18. FORMER AMP SOCIETY BUILDING
Corner Itchen & Tees Sts (HPT I)

18. Former AMP Society Building
The AMP Society's 'Amicus' still adorns a building that started as a drapery and ended up as a private club.

Drapers Hood and Shennan began in Wansbeck Street in the early 1860s. In 1871, as the retail district seeped away, they commissioned Forrester & Lemon to design their new Itchen Street shop, which they extended along Tees Street in 1875. Forrester & Lemon returned in 1885–86 to remodel it in simplified Victorian Italianate style for the Australian Mutual Provident (AMP) Society. AMP's 'Amicus' marble statue still adorns the intersection, but the insurer moved out long ago. The Ministry of Agriculture and Fisheries once worked here but now it houses an art studio, health facility and its long-term inhabitant, the North Otago Club.

☞ ☞ *Return to the Visitor Centre, to conclude this section of our walk.*

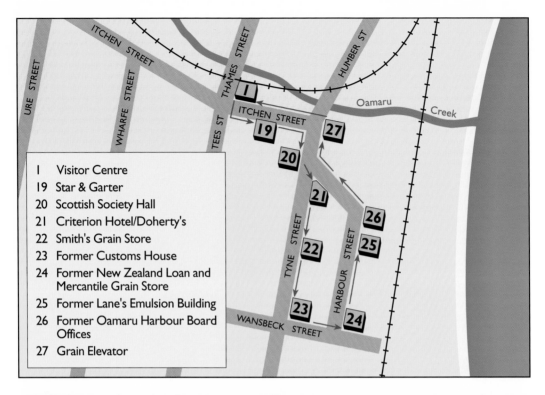

I	Visitor Centre
19	Star & Garter
20	Scottish Society Hall
21	Criterion Hotel/Doherty's
22	Smith's Grain Store
23	Former Customs House
24	Former New Zealand Loan and Mercantile Grain Store
25	Former Lane's Emulsion Building
26	Former Oamaru Harbour Board Offices
27	Grain Elevator

19. Star & Garter
The Star & Garter, Oamaru's first large stone hotel, greets the dawn. The Star had to find other uses after prohibitionists voted Oamaru 'dry' early last century. Further down the street are Corner Collectibles and, across the road, the Woolstore.

☞ ☞ *From the Visitor Centre turn into Itchen Street and cross to the Star & Garter.*

19. STAR & GARTER
Itchen Street (HPT II)

Andrew Baker's wooden Northern Hotel was doing a roaring trade in 1867 when Robert Lawson gave Richard Jones half of this elegant hotel, the first of Oamaru's elaborately decorated masonry hotels. Jones had bought the first building on the site, Hertslet's Accommodation House (1858) and renamed it the Star & Garter. His timing was good, for the hotel opened just as the new Itchen Street cutting started to pull business north from Wansbeck and Tyne Streets. Dunedin coaches soon forsook the Northern for the Star & Garter, which housed the hotel and the Masonic Hall. The western extension opened in 1868 and in the mid 1870s the hotel expanded into the Masonic Hall space when the brethren built their own premises in Wansbeck Street (page 48). A plaque honours the site's Masonic connection.

In 1915 fire badly damaged the hotel, which was not repaired fully for some time. Like the Brydone, the roofline of the Star & Garter was once as elaborately decorated as the restored Criterion (page 39), with a row of fine stone urns above the balustrade. Nevertheless, the Star & Garter fared better than the Tyne Street hotels that we will visit soon. Since the First World War it has housed clubs and theatres – the RSA, Lyric Theatre, Peter Pan Theatre, Manhattan clothing factory and more recently the Oamaru Repertory Theatre. Behind it is a stable, probably built in 1861, Oamaru's oldest surviving building.

The Woolstore (left, rear) and Corner Collectibles (right, foreground). Shops and a weekend market have brought fresh life to the precinct.

☞ ☞ *Continue to the Itchen/Tyne Street intersection. In our photograph (left) the contrast in height of the Woolstore (left, 1881, Connell and Clowes' Grain Store, HPT II) and the corner store (right) founded by James Bee in the mid 1860s, reminds us that this side of Tyne Street is the older. Corner Collectables, as Bee's is now known, and the neighbouring Easymade Marmalade building (8 Tyne Street), typify the first masonry structures that replaced the late 1850s single-storey wooden merchants' warehouses. With his own bakery and wine and spirit licences, Bee supplied everyone from sailors to farmers and settlers. Continue south to the Scottish Society Hall.*

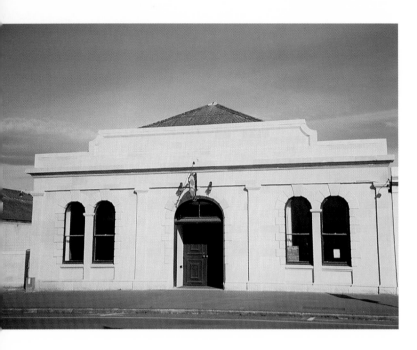

20. SCOTTISH SOCIETY HALL

Tyne Street (HPT II)

This simple limestone building is one of the oldest easily viewed buildings in the precinct. It probably dates from 1864, when the eastern side of Tyne Street was the commercial heart of the town. In the days before specialised retail shops, Traill & Roxby, Dalgety, Rattray & Co., Hassell & Co. and Henry France traded from general warehouses such as this. Rattray & Co. arrived on Tyne Street in 1860 and just four years later felt confident enough to rebuild in stone. Later owners included grain merchants and auctioneers, Fleming & Hedley, and then the New Zealand Loan & Mercantile Co. Since 1929, the North Otago Scottish Society has owned the building, which continues to host shows and other events. What you see reflects changing fashions. During the 1950s the Society kept up with the times by plastering over the facade. Forty years later crumbling plaster and another change in taste prompted it to chip back its earlier handiwork to reveal the battered original limestone. The new 'old' facade re-emerged in 1997.

20. Scottish Society Hall
The Scottish Society Hall is the third of these early former merchants' warehouses. It is often used for flower shows and concerts.

☞ ☞ *South of here the foundry has made its presence felt on Tyne Street's western side, which we will skip. Some early buildings survive, most notably the former Union Bank of Australia (1878, HPT I, right), 14 Tyne Street; its acclaimed Venetian palazzo Renaissance facade has been cleaned but the building was altered for squash courts decades ago. We will now cross Tyne Street to the pub.*

21. CRITERION HOTEL/DOHERTY'S

3 Tyne Street (HPT I)

21. Criterion Hotel/Doherty's
The Criterion spent most of last century as first a humble boarding house and then skin buyer's store but it has now been restored as the flagship for the historic precinct. On the left is part of the Woolstore.

In 1874 the newly subdivided west side of Tyne Street, the 'Harbour Board block', was thrown open for lease. First up were the grain stores and the harbour board's offices, but in 1877 hotelier William Gillespie built the Criterion on this key corner site. In the same year that it was reported that no Oamaru hotel possessed a bath, Forrester and Lemon gave Gillespie this urn, pinnacle and tympana-encrusted hotel to rival the Star & Garter. The ground floor of the adjoining building served as a woolstore and offices for Connell and Clowes, while its upper floor was part of the Criterion. The Cri soon fell foul of the prohibitionists, who voted the district 'dry' in 1905. A year later the town's 10 hotels closed their bars. The Criterion, like the rest, survived as a private boarding house until about 1940 when it passed into the hands of the local foundry, with the southern extension housing wool and skin buyer Jock Doherty. Interest in the Criterion picked up in the 1980s when it formed part of the backdrop to 'Pictures', a film about the Burton Brothers, and was registered by the Historic Places Trust in 1987. Then the Oamaru Whitestone Civic Trust took over. It put the decoration back on the balustrade in 1998 and for the first time in over 90 years it was possible to legally quench your thirst here.

21. Criterion Hotel/Doherty's

☞ ☞ *Walk a few metres south to the tall building.*

22. SMITH'S GRAIN STORE
Tyne Street (HPT I)

The Historic Places Trust describes James Johnston's creation as 'probably the most ornamental grain store in the country'. Architect Chris Cochran considers it important nationally as 'a sophisticated and rare example of a building in the Italian palazzo style'. The *Oamaru Mail* of the day also doffed its cap, praising this 'temple of art' but Joseph Smith's store was up for sale in 'mortgage alley' by 1884. The upstairs was used for church meetings, a roller skating rink and then as a dance hall. But it was the presence of the *Oamaru Mail* from 1906 until 1970 that really made the building significant. Colonial Oamaru had several papers, beginning with the *Oamaru Times and Waitaki Reporter* (1864). The established *North Otago Times* became a morning daily in 1876, followed closely by the new *Evening Mail*, which, under George Jones, changed its name to the *Oamaru Mail* and slugged it out with the *Times* until the latter ceased publication in 1932. The *Mail* moved to new premises in Coquet Street in 1970. At one time the company also controlled the *Southland Evening News*, but the *Oamaru Mail* is now itself part of a larger group and has been reduced to Monday-Friday publication since 1993. Joiners replaced compositors in the 1970s and in 1992 the Whitestone Civic Trust bought Smith's for conservation (completed in 2001).

Opposite, top:
22. Smith's Grain Store (1882) Joseph Smith's Union Stores, better known as Smith's Grain Store, opened its doors as the grain boom collapsed. For over 60 years it housed the Oamaru Mail. Here it flanks the Union Offices (left) and the NMA building.

Artists and craftspeople have breathed new life into the precinct.

☞ ☞ *Walk south to the Wansbeck Street intersection. East Tyne Street presents a virtually unbroken line of Victorian buildings, now mostly restored. The next pair after Smith's both had long associations with stock and station agents, NMA (1875) and Darling and McDowell Ltd (built 1889 as the Exchange Chambers for George Sumpter).*

23. FORMER CUSTOMS HOUSE
Corner Tyne and Wansbeck Streets (HPT I)

Alexander Watson completed this no-nonsense Forrester & Lemon design for the Customs Department in 1884, just as Sumpter Wharf opened to serve the meat trade to London. Customs staff had little time to enjoy their new quarters, though, because in 1887 in a complicated deal, the county council vacated its building in favour of the girls' high school and moved in here. When the county departed in 1905, the Oamaru Technical School moved in and Customs did not get back in until 1925, after which it shared the premises with others until 1966, when Oamaru ceased to be an entry port. The Royal Antediluvian Order of Buffaloes owned the building from 1972 until 1980. Then the Historic Places Trust bought it, conserving, covenanting and selling the building to the North Otago Art Society eight years later.

23. Former Customs House
Oamaru was declared a Port of
Entry in 1861 and remained
one until 1966, seven years
before the last overseas cargo
arrived from Australia. These
days the North Otago Art
Society uses it to display and
sell members' work.

☞ ☞ Turn left into Wansbeck Street and walk to the big grain store at the end of Harbour Street.

24. FORMER NEW ZEALAND LOAN AND MERCANTILE GRAIN STORE

14 Harbour Street (HPT I)

They built confidently even as the grain boom ebbed and the colony sank into depression. Those jutting quoins at the southern end show that the original owners had even grander plans for the huge three-storey, 100,000-sack capacity warehouse building, commissioned in 1882 by the 'Loan and Merc', as the powerful company was often called. Architects Dennison & Grant lightened its bulk with pleasing decorative flourishes such as the twisted ropework around the windows. It is one of New Zealand's most important historic warehouses. In 1961 The New Zealand Loan and Mercantile Company merged with Dalgety. The Civic Trust now owns the building, which serves a furniture factory. If you have time, have a look around the back, where the loading bays once loaded grain into railway wagons for the short journey to the port.

24. Loan & Mercantile Store
Big though the 'Loan & Merc' store is, the projecting quoins show that its owners originally had even bigger plans for it. Decorative details around the windows and doors (above) lighten the store's massive bulk.

☞ ☞ Walk north along Harbour Street. Our photo (opposite, top) looks north along this street to the part-corrugated iron side of Woolstore. From left to right are our next stop, the former Lane's Emulsion Building, and then two Forrester & Lemon grain stores, the 1876 J. & T. Meek Store and the two-storey Sumpter's Grain Store of 1878 (both HPT II). As we walk up the street we pass on our right James McGill's design for Anderson & Mowat (1878) and Forrester & Lemon's 1882 store for Neil Brothers (both HPT II). Stop at the gable-roofed greystone building (opposite).

Opposite:
25. Lane's Emulsion Building
The little gabled, greystone Lane's Emulsion building now houses a bakery and organics shop. To its right are J. & T. Meek's (1875) and Sumpter's (1878) grain stores.

25. FORMER LANE'S EMULSION BUILDING
2 Harbour Street (HPT II)

'Welcome to Oamaru, the Home of Lane's Emulsion', the signs said. From these premises Edward Lane inflicted Lane's Emulsion, a vile-tasting, foul-smelling cod liver oil remedy on generations of generally ungrateful Australasian children. 'It's Famous Because It's Good', the wordy, worthy and faintly homoerotic packaging assured customers, who bought salvation from coughs, colds, consumption, bronchitis, whooping cough, asthma, la grippe (influenza), pneumonia and whatever else ailed them. This local rough-hewed greystone warehouse is a rare exception to the limestone streetscape. Lane's had been built to a simple design as a grain store for A.H. Maude. It became Lane's factory in 1908 after he outgrew his Tees Street premises (the little shop, No. 2 Tees, still stands next to the southern boundary of St Luke's). A skilled salesman, Lane opened a branch of the business in Melbourne in the 1920s. Local chemists Crombie & Price took over the Lane's Medicine Company in 1969 and kept churning out the stuff until 1984, when Aucklanders acquired the rights.

☞ ☞ *Walk next door.*

26. FORMER OAMARU HARBOUR BOARD OFFICES

2 Harbour St (HPT I)

If any institution built Oamaru it was the Oamaru Harbour Board. The top portion of its common seal depicted its dream, a ship snugly moored behind the breakwater, a steam crane busy at work behind it. In the lower panel were stacked the exports of the young economy, bags of wheat, bales of wool and blocks of stone. Suspended above them all, though, was the Golden Fleece, symbolising both the promise held by the hinterland and the solidity proclaimed by the town's Greek Revival public buildings.

Harbour boards were created under 1870 legislation to take over the duties of the provincial governments' harbour departments in towns that could afford them. Many could not and many were little more than the local road board or county council doubling up as a harbour authority. Oamaru, formed in 1874, was one of the more substantial. Nevertheless, it overstretched itself and by defaulting on interest payments in 1891 it 'made the name of Oamaru an unpleasant one in the ears of London money-lenders' and caused the *Financial Times* to mutter about 'the recklessness or worse of colonial borrowers'. It did trade itself out of the red and survived until 1978, four years after the last ship used the port. You will find a plaque setting out its milestones near the breakwater (see page 51).

If any Oamaru building stands for Thomas Forrester, it is this delightful little Venetian-influenced building. A draftsman, engineer and self-taught architect, Forrester was also a skilled administrator and gifted amateur scholar. Until his death Forrester worked for the harbour board as its secretary, inspector of works and later engineer. His discovery that the sea floor could be dredged kept Oamaru in the vital 'Home' (UK) trade. The Oamaru Harbour Board met here from 1876 until 1978. After serving the perfume company working in the neighbouring Lane's Building, it is now home to the Oamaru Whitestone Civic Trust.

☞ ☞ *Walk up Harbour Street to Tyne, then head north, past the Wool Store. Cross the rail line and stop in front of the tall building set back slightly from the street.*

26. Former Oamaru Harbour Board Offices
Oamaru's most important Forrester & Lemon building is the one that Thomas Forrester designed for his employer, the Oamaru Harbour Board. It owned and tenanted the land on which the neighbouring grain stores were built.

27. Grain Elevator
Seen from Tyne Street, it is an imposing and distinctive building. From a new garden on the northern side you can see how much of the building was destroyed by the 1920 fire. Compare it with the historic photograph on p. 11.

27. GRAIN ELEVATOR
Set back, northern end of Tyne Street (HPT II)

The New Zealand Elevator Company's (later J. & T. Meek's) grain elevator once dominated the skyline. Consider the statistics. The ponderous mansard-roofed structure was 21 metres high, 20 metres wide and 50 metres long. There was 5,100 metres of floor space and the interior – reached through doors wide enough to fit railway wagons – had 38 large wooden storage bins, each 6.4 metres deep. The latest American-style technology let five workers run the complex at full capacity. That was not often. Unfortunately for the Meeks, who also owned a flour mill (page 32) and the grain store beside Lane's Emulsion (page 42), their unique elevator was a white(stone) elephant. It opened just as farmers switched to meat and wool and while North Otago still kept growing grain (it processes most of our birdseed) production fell and the building struggled to earn its keep. In January 1920 fire burnt out the top storey, collapsing the roof. The owners made repairs but did not rebuild the top two storeys or the eastern end, which looks like a dinosaur chomped it. Like many of its neighbours, it spent recent decades storing materials for the foundry.

☞ ☞ *That completes this walk. Return to the Visitor Centre or refresh yourself at the pub or cafes.*

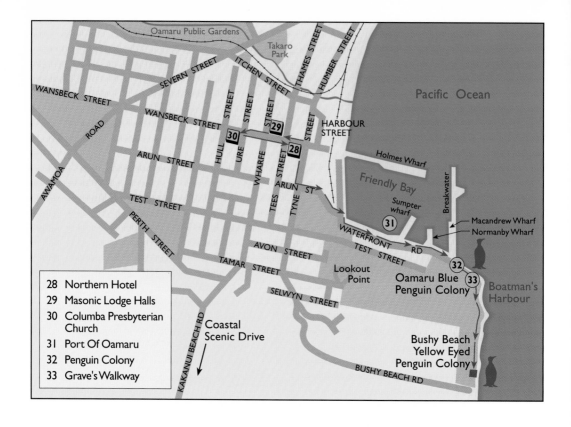

Oamaru Public Gardens

Takaro Park

Pacific Ocean

WANSBECK STREET

SEVERN STREET

ITCHEN STREET

THAMES STREET

HUMBER STREET

WANSBECK STREET

ROAD

HULL STREET

URE STREET

WHARFE STREET

TEES STREET

TYNE STREET

HARBOUR STREET

Holmes Wharf

Friendly Bay

ARUN STREET

30

29

28

ARUN ST

Sumpter wharf

Breakwater

AWAMOA

TEST STREET

PERTH STREET

31

WATERFRONT RD

TEST STREET

Macandrew Wharf

Normanby Wharf

AVON STREET

TAMAR STREET

Lookout Point

32

33

Boatman's Harbour

SELWYN STREET

Oamaru Blue Penguin Colony

KAKANUI BEACH RD

Coastal Scenic Drive

Bushy Beach Yellow Eyed Penguin Colony

BUSHY BEACH RD

28 Northern Hotel
29 Masonic Lodge Halls
30 Columba Presbyterian Church
31 Port Of Oamaru
32 Penguin Colony
33 Grave's Walkway

Below: Oamaru Harbour seen from Test Street. Holmes Wharf, the main wharf, runs east from Friendly Bay (left).

28. NORTHERN HOTEL
cnr Tyne St/Wansbeck Streets (HPT II)

28. Northern Hotel
The Northern bears the traces
of its chequered past.

Why, you may ask, since we have been walking southwards, is central Oamaru's southernmost hotel called the *Northern*? The name goes back to 1860. Then, anyone wading ashore from the Victorian equivalent of white water rafting – a hair-raising ride through the Oamaru breakers in one of Traill and Roxby's surfboats – would have welcomed the sight of Otago's northern-most hotel, which was also the terminus for coaches from Dunedin. The first two-storey hotel was a simpler Baltic Pine version of the present building, designed by Forrester and Lemon in Italianate style for G.H. Amos in 1879. Allegedly the 'squatters' hotel', it offered five bedrooms on the ground floor, seventeen above, and did a fair trade until 1894 when the prohibitionists, in the first stage of their campaign, snatched away the licences of several hotels, including the Northern's.

After struggling along as a private hotel and boarding place, the Northern became part of the foundry, gaining a massive concrete block blight on its Wansbeck Street rear and an open-air scrapheap on its southern edge. Shabby and keeping poor company, the wonderfully historic Northern continues to survive by the limestone skin of its teeth.

☞ ☞ *On your left as you make your way up Wansbeck Street are three battered terrace shops (1879, HPT II), built surprisingly long after the shopping district started moving away. Their big glass windows contrast with the earlier warehouses that we saw around the Itchen/Tyne Street intersection.*

☞ ☞ *The next two places will explain why Wansbeck made such a poor main entrance for the town. Cross the Wansbeck/Tees Street intersection and stop in front of the Masonic Lodges on the right.*

29. MASONIC LODGE HALLS

(1933, front, and 1876, rear)

Wansbeck Street (not registered)

Like friendly societies, volunteer fire brigades, military units and bands, the lodges supplemented colonial pubs in creating and strengthening male social and business networks. The Oddfellows (Manchester Unity) set up in Oamaru in 1864 and followed by the Masonic lodge, Lodge Waitaki IIII E.C., a year later. Soon there were more lodges, clubs and friendly societies. The Wansbeck Street lodges testify to the 'Craft's' power here. The front building, built in 1933, is one of the town's few stripped classical structures. It is a substantial and dignified masonry building with one of New Zealand's most striking interiors, almost worth signing up just to see inside. Behind it, almost unnoticed, is another big building. Built to Thomas Glass's design in 1876, it became the refectory for the complex in the 1930s. Blocked in front by the 1933 building and walled off around the sides, it can be reached only by going through the front building!

☞ ☞ *Continue up Wansbeck Street to Columba Church.*

29. Masonic Lodges
Look carefully and you will see the edge of the 1876 lodge, almost completely obscured by the 1933 building.

30. Columba Church
Columba Church dominates this stretch of Wansbeck Street, a boxy contrast to the town's more common Gothic churches. Note the big houses in the neighbouring streets. Colonial middle class families prized the sunny north-facing slopes of the South Hill for their good sea views (below).

30. COLUMBA PRESBYTERIAN CHURCH

Corner Wansbeck & Ure Streets (HPT II)

If you begin to puff and pant, you will understand why Wansbeck Street was not the ideal main entrance to Oamaru in the days of bullock carts. As soon as the gentler Itchen Street connection linked Severn and Thames streets, businesses began to drift away, leaving the sunny slopes of the South Hill to develop as a residential area. Columba Church (dedicated to Saint Columba) was Oamaru's second Presbyterian church (for the first, St Paul's (1873) see page 55). In a break with their previous ecclesiastical work, Forrester & Lemon turned out this plain Basilica-style classical church capable of seating 800. The four Doric columns flanked by the hefty square Doric pillars and the massive pediment give the northern façade an imposing presence but, in all but size, the austere Columba conforms most fully to the Presbyterian Church's Scottish addiction to the simple rectangular 'preaching box'. Ironically, though, in a town as full of classical columns as Oamaru, Columba looks more like a bank than a church! The building was extensively modified in 1921 for a new vestibule, gallery and organ chamber and again in 1935, when Doric pillars were installed to delineate the exterior aisles and also to enhance the beginning of the apse.

☞ ☞ *Return to the Northern Hotel, then walk south along Tyne Street to the Arun Street intersection. On the way you will pass an old wool and skin buyer's premises that was originally House's buggy and seed cleaning equipment emporium and assembler. Follow the footpath down to the harbour. On your right are King George Park and Whitestone Lodge, the former Victoria Home (1897), shafted several decades ago by a modern extension thrust into the centre of its dignified frontage.*

A Conference Lines freighter loads cargo at Holmes Wharf between the wars.
North Otago Museum

31. PORT OF OAMARU (1872–1907)

Waterfront Road (HPT II, breakwater only)

The prosperity that created the white stone buildings we have seen rested on the Port of Oamaru, now New Zealand's only intact Victorian/Edwardian deep-sea port. Oamaru was one of the so-called 'protein ports' that from the 1880s interlinked the New Zealand and British economies. The largest wharf is Holmes Wharf. This was built about a century ago to keep pace with a new generation of 10,000-ton overseas freighters on the North Mole (1880), a long, slender finger of rock that protected the wharves from northerly surges. Named after the harbour board chairman, Holmes Wharf kept Oamaru in the 'Home trade' until 1940. It opened in 1907, the last and largest design of Thomas Forrester, who died a year earlier. Running between Holmes Wharf and Waterfront Road are the remains of an old art deco esplanade, completed in 1939 by the Friendly Bay Improvement Society. For many years its Christmas carnivals were a summer highlight.

Sumpter Wharf.

A bollard and the Robert and Betsy*'s mast are relics from the sailing ship era.*

The remnants of the Ramsay Extension stretch out from the breakwater.

Artists and community groups now use the old Red Sheds (right).

The south side of the port is older. Walk along the old stone seawall to Sumpter Wharf, the big wooden wharf with two old wooden sheds near its entrance. In 1884, when it opened, you might have found the *Elderslie*, the first refrigerated steamer designed to run between New Zealand and Britain, or the meat trade's pioneer, the *Dunedin*, a frequent caller. Big British tramps loaded grain to feed the army's horses during the Boer War and shipping continued to use it up until the Second World War.

Walk east past the little wooden jetties, which are recent. By the slipway is a relic of Oamaru's notorious shipwreck days, a mast from the *Robert and Betsy*, a brigantine wrecked in 1862. Bought by beachmaster Captain William Sewell, it served as a signal mast, then stood for many decades in Tyne Street before coming here in the 1990s. The next wharf, Normanby Wharf, a wide concrete wharf with berths on three sides, was completed in 1878. Running off its east side is another concrete quay, the Cross Wharf, used by Scott's Own Sea Scouts for many years. The group takes its name from Antarctic explorer, Captain Scott, whose ship *Terra Nova* landed a boat in the early hours of 8 February 1913 to telegraph the dramatic news of Scott's death. On the right across the road are the former Oamaru Harbour Board quarry and the board's rustic red corrugated iron workshops.

Finally, by the penguin colony, we reach the breakwater. On its inner side is Macandrew Wharf (1875), named after Otago Superintendent James Macandrew. It does not look much, but in the 1870s shipping fought for space alongside it. Although seas could sweep wharf and breakwater before the latter was raised in the 1930s, Macandrew Wharf signalled the end of Oamaru's shipwreck era. Walkem and Peyman and Miller & Smillie built the 564-metre long breakwater in stages between 1872 and 1884, despite often daunting seas. Even incomplete, it transformed the

port's appalling safety record. The landward end was raised between the wars and further altered a decade ago. The rocky spur off the seaward side is the stunted remnant of the Ramsay Extension, built during the Depression to provide a sheltered shipping channel out to deeper water. It had advanced 220 metres when money ran out and work stopped in 1944, the overseas shipping it was designed to serve gone forever. It has been crumbling away ever since.

32. PENGUIN COLONY

Seaward end of Waterfront Road (not registered)

Although the blue penguin, or korara, is the world's smallest, just 250–300 mm tall, and weighing a kilogram, it is also New Zealand's most common. Think of blues as maritime sparrows, for they are not afraid to build their nests in house basements or other human structures during the breeding season and artificial lights do not deter them. They are common nocturnal visitors to built-up areas such as Wellington, where road signs warn motorists to watch out for them, and Oamaru, where enterprising locals have made them a major visitor attraction at the historic Oamaru Harbour Board quarry, which was turned over to the penguin colony in 1992.

Since then, increasing numbers of tourists have been viewing the penguins as they come ashore just after sunset each evening. For about an hour each night these small birds make their way ashore up the steep banks and across a virtual parade area as they head for the wooden nesting boxes that have been built for them on the quarry floor. Oamaru blues with young chicks may have swum as much as twenty-five kilometres off shore and travelled up to seventy-five kilometres during their day's hunt for food.

The visitor centre opened in December 2001 and the viewing stand in 2002. Check the centre's display room, webcam and notices for the latest information about penguin activity, numbers and viewing times, or ask at the Thames Street Visitor Centre. Numbers peak in the breeding season (September–January) but there are always some penguins here year round. Blues come ashore at another penguin reserve north of Holmes Wharf and from time to time other penguin breeds – crested, erect crested and Fiordland penguins – also make an appearance at the quarry colony.

Blue penguins at a nest box on the Oamaru foreshore.
Dave Houston

Grave's Walkway at Boatman's Harbour. Take the track down to the shore to view the pillow lava (below). Isabella Harrex

The remains of the small lighthouse can be found near the observation post just above Boatman's Harbour.

33. GRAVE'S WALKWAY
Seaward end of Waterfront Road (HPT II)

Grave's Walkway honours William George Grave, who raised funds for one of the places on our first walk, the South African War Memorial. Fittingly, he features in our last stop. In the 1920s he laboured to form this track, or marine parade as it was called. The work was arduous – in some places the cliffs were so steep that he had to lower himself by rope from the cliff tops. In the 1930s, in declining health, Grave supervised the relief workers who completed the job. Slips have closed it for lengthy periods over the decades. The two-kilometre walkway offers some spectacular views out over the sea but is steep, can be slippery in the wet and may not suit people with disabilities or a fear of heights. It is closed an hour before dusk each day.

Sunny mornings are best and a low tide will give the option of walking back along the beach. On a good day you may see spotted shags or the occasional sea lion wallowing around in the waves. Seals bask on the rocks below. A side extension above Boatman's Harbour can take you up to the World War Two coastal defence site, where a former American five-inch gun protected the port from 1942 until early 1945. You can also see the former observation post and the abandoned lighthouse. Do take the track down to the cove at Boatman's Harbour, where at low tide you will see the unusual volcanic structures known as pillow lava. They were formed 40–50 million years ago when a submarine volcano spewed lava out over the seabed in long interconnecting fingers. The seawater cooled the hot lava to form a solid glassy shell. That cooling process continued inside the fingers, contracting as it did and producing the radial fractures you can see today.

Morning light bathes the loess cliffs at Bushy Beach.

Take the path back up to the walkway and continue south to Bushy Beach, where there is another penguin colony, this time of the larger and rarer yellow-eyed penguin, or hoiho (ask the Visitor Centre for more information). You can return either by retracing your steps along the walkway or by taking the Bushy Beach Road, which connects with upper Tyne Street.

Oamaru has many other interesting places. This chapter offers a selection of some of the more notable ones in and around the town. First we take a walk, from the freezing works to the Basilica. This will take about 20–25 minutes, starting from the Grain Elevator. Alternatively, you may decide to drive.

☞ ☞ *From the Grain Elevator, cross the Humber Street bridge at the northern end of Tyne Street and head north.*

FORMER FREEZING WORKS
Humber Street (HPT II)

You will have to gaze across the railway line to see this simple utilitarian structure. Location was always its undoing, cramped between the sea and the rail lines. The New Zealand Refrigerating Company commissioned Forrester & Lemon to design this works, with its classic 'sawtooth' industrial roofline, in 1885–86. It served until just before the First World War when the Pukeuri works opened north of the town. More or less a first generation freezing works frozen in time, its historic significance probably exceeds its old Historic Places Trust registration status.

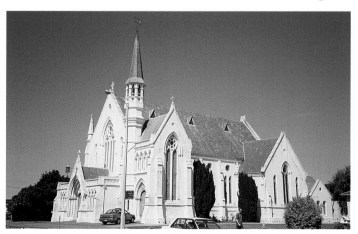

☞ ☞ *Keep heading north. On the right are the remains of the old gasworks. On the left in Coquet Street you will see the spire of another Forrester & Lemon Presbyterian Church, St Paul's (left, 1873).*

Oamaru Railway Station.

OAMARU RAILWAY STATION
Humber Street (HPT I)

Ironically, until recently, travellers could also enter the 'Whitestone City' through a highly elaborate *wooden* railway station. Oamaru's first permanent station (1873) lurked at the foot of Wansbeck Street, a sensible location when the port was the town's front door to the world. A replacement was being called for within five years, but all the town got was an upgrade to cope with the completion of the South Island main trunk from Christchurch to Invercargill in early 1879.

This station dates from 1900 and both it and its location are significant since they signalled the final demise of Tyne Street's prosperity, by accelerating the business centre's drift north. Rail heritage buffs call this carpenter gothic colossus a 'Vintage Troup' station, which means that it was built in the first decade of the 20th century to the design of railway architect George Troup. Note the trademark half-timbered construction and Marseilles tile roof. Troup earned the nickname 'Gingerbread George', for his love of ornamentation. His 1906 Dunedin extravaganza exemplifies this, but Oamaru's elaborate porte-cochere hints at things to come. Oamaru's 700-seat dining room was the largest in the South Island until it closed in 1967. The railcars, 'cabbage trains', and bustling refreshment rooms are just a memory, as are the single men's huts across the street, but in 2001 after a decade of shabby neglect by private 'enterprise', the old station was bought by the Totara Hotels Charitable Foundation for the Civic Trust for restoration. Passenger trains stopped calling early in 2002, but the station and its long platforms speak eloquently of Oamaru's importance to the main trunk line.

Meldrum's Bakery.

☞ ☞ *Go north, turn left into Usk Street and cross Thames Street and head towards the Roman Catholic Basilica. On the left is the spruce but sad stump of Meldrum's Bakery (HPT II), butchered to provide access to a fast-food carpark.*

ST PATRICK'S ROMAN CATHOLIC BASILICA

64 Reed St (HPT I)

Welcome to the heart of Catholic Oamaru. This massive structure is the work of Father John McKay, energetic parish priest over the entire construction period, and architect Francis William Petre. It was completed in three stages – the nave in 1894, the Corinthian portico and flanking domes in 1903 and the remainder in 1918. They nicknamed Petre 'Lord Concrete', so you can be sure that a concrete core lurks behind the Oamaru Stone. Inside the nave an ingeniously designed clerestory and the big dome deluge brilliant light over the sanctuary. Go inside – that dome, the coffered Renaissance ceiling and the strangely medieval and Eurocentric Stations of the Cross merit close inspection.

While you are here, walk north along the Reed Street footpath to admire the rest of the precinct. Alongside the Basilica sits the simple Presbytery (HPT II, believed to have been built about the turn of the century, although the upper storey was added about 20–30 years later). Beside it is the chapel from the former St. Thomas's Girls' High School and the former Rosary Convent (1901, HPT II), now a retirement home – which also has its own attractive chapel (1920) at the northern end of the complex.

St Patrick's dome rises up over Oamaru. Cape Wanbrow is to the right.

☞ ☞ *Waitaki Boys' High School is the next visit. It is about eight minutes' drive or a 45-minute walk to the north end of town. A sealed bicycle track starts at the northern end of Humber Street.*

Waitaki Boys' High School
The Central Block (left) and
South Wing (right) date from
1905 and 1912 respectively,
although the latter was rebuilt
in 1921 after fire damage.

WAITAKI BOY'S HIGH SCHOOL

Waitaki Avenue (HPT I Main Block and Hall of Memories)

In 1878 Parliament legislated for Waitaki Boys' High, largely thanks to Samuel Shrimski's efforts. H.J. Miller, who succeeded Shrimski as chairman, dreamed of an antipodean Eton but irked Oamaruvians, who objected to public reserves being used to benefit the few. The fee-charging, classics-dominated school opened in 1883 with just nineteen pupils. It compounded its sins by setting up a haughty two kilometres distance north of the borough boundary. This incited Columba Church's Dr James McGregor to campaign to close it and replace it with a less élite school in town. McGregor, both 'intellectually a Triton among the Oamaru minnows' and 'a violent and intractable partisan', shared the Free Church Scottish passion for equality of opportunity in education. An 1886 parliamentary inquiry saved the school, but as Waitaki's historian admitted, 'the quarrel did the school no good. For many years it continued to be regarded as a class institution for the sons of the well-to-do'.

Frank Milner's portrait adorns
the south wall of the Hall of
Memories.

Some token free places muted criticism. Nevertheless, Waitaki became famous for imperial enthusiasm and interest in international affairs during the lengthy rectorship (1906–44) of Frank Milner, the *Dictionary of New Zealand Biography's* pick as the country's 'leading secondary school principal and educationalist'. Milner, or 'The Man' as he was known, made Waitaki 'not just a school from which the sons of middle-class New Zealand would emerge as well-educated, healthy-minded, responsible citizens: they would be sons of the Empire as well, cells of political decency in a world that sorely needed the Arnoldian virtues of tradition, taste and liberalism'. But not socialism. Milner's imperialism, increasingly anachronistic in its condemnation of leftists, nationalists and anti-conscriptionists, led him to offer himself as a National Party candidate for the postponed 1941 election. Not surprisingly, some Labour parents refused to send their sons to this 'upper class school'.

The school's older architecture reflects its earlier Etonian and imperial aspirations. Forrester & Lemon's Rectory dates from 1883. The Central Block was built in 1905 and the South Wing (rebuilt in 1921 after a fire) joined it in 1912. The Hall of Memories, one of the most extraordinary buildings in New Zealand, can excite strong, often conflicting emotions in visitors. One hundred and nineteen of the 700 old boys who served during the First World War had died, so the 1920 Easter Reunion decided to erect a special hall of memories. John Forrester inspected many of the English-style public school halls before returning to design this Perpendicular Gothic structure. Governor-General Jellicoe laid the foundation stone in 1923 and HRH the Duke of York performed the official opening ceremony on 16 March 1927.

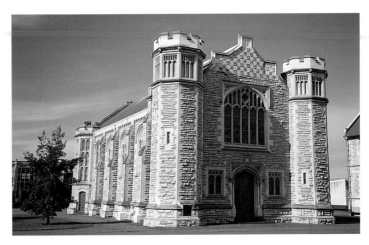

The Duke of York opened the Hall of Memories in 1927. Its interior is full of flags, trophies, crests and other memorabilia. Visitors are welcome during school hours, but call at the school office first to collect the Munsters-sized key. A detailed self-guide pamphlet explains all the flags, pennants, plaques, trophies, portraits and stained glass windows.

☞ ☞ *The next visits are to two Historic Places Trust properties, both once part of the New Zealand and Australian Land Company's huge Totara Estate. Ask the Visitor Centre for Totara Estate's seasonal opening times. Clark's Flourmill is not open regularly, but may be visited by arrangement with Totara Estate staff. Drive or take a tour to these properties.*

TOTARA ESTATE, OAMARU
State Highway 1.8 km south of Oamaru (HPT I)

Few historic places can match the significance of Totara Estate, birthplace of the New Zealand frozen meat trade. Before refrigeration only wool could be exported. Early pastoralists often erected yards at the edges of cliffs, drove old sheep into them, knocked them on the head, then tossed the carcasses over the edge. There was just too much meat for colonials to eat, even when they ate it three meals a day. This prompted the New Zealand manager of the huge New Zealand and Australian Land Company's estates, William Soltau Davidson, to experiment. In 1881, while the Albion Line fitted a Bell-Coleman plant to its ship *Dunedin*, at Totara the Land Company added a slaughterhouse to these 1868 farm buildings. Here Davidson and Totara manager Thomas Brydone supervised the slaughtering and the dispatch of the carcasses by rail to Port Chalmers. They were frozen aboard the *Dunedin*, which left the port on 15 February 1882 and landed the cargo in London three months later in perfect condition. This was the beginning of a social, political and economic transformation. 'A new economy and society was created', the *New Zealand Historical Atlas* noted. It was 'one of sheep bred for meat as much as for wool, of owner-occupier farms rather than stations with large numbers of hands, of freezing works and their associated communities, and of ports, some of the activities of which were dominated by this industry'.

Totara Estate
The stables housed many of the estate's horses, their harnesses and a groom, who decorated his walls with newspapers that you can still see.

Bottom left: Looking from the men's quarters back to the stables. The interior of the men's quarters (below) shows the very basic living conditions 'enjoyed' by colonial farmhands.

In 1980 the Historic Places Trust, helped by the meat industry, restored the buildings and opened them to the public precisely 100 years after the *Dunedin*'s historic sailing. The slaughterhouse had not survived, but you can still inspect its concrete floor and blood gutter beneath the new display shelter constructed in 2002. Most of the other buildings – the men's quarters and workshop, carcass shed, stables and granary – survive and are fitted out with interesting displays on the estate, rural labour and on the meat trade. For the fit, the nearby Brydone Memorial makes a pleasant 30–40 minute climb.

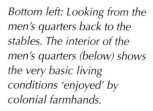

Clark's Flourmill
Clark's was built in two parts, the Oamaru stone section in 1866 and the corrugated iron store in 1872. Water power from the Kakanui River came down a millrace and it is said that a single man could run the mill (although up to six usually worked here). Much of the nineteenth century machinery is still here.

CLARK'S FLOURMILL, MAHENO
State Highway 1, near Maheno (HPT II)

Flourmilling was a important industry for North Otago for over a century from the 1860s. Flour mills ground locally-grown wheat, Oamaru warehouses stored it by the shipload, and at times the stuff comprised about a quarter of the port's coastal exports. In 1866 this mill, which drew water from a specially constructed race, was built for Matthew Holmes and Henry Campbell, owners of the huge Totara Estate, which they sold to the New Zealand and Australian Land Company a year later. The Land Company leased it out. The Clark brothers, Alex, David and Robert, took it over from the Land Company in 1901 and extended the building. Alex later restyled it Clark's Milling Co. Ltd, in partnership with his sons. The Clarks converted it to electricity but left most of the older plant. In 1977 the Historic Places Trust bought what it described as the country's last water-powered mill with much of its early machinery intact. Big bread was spent restoring buildings and machinery, but industry changes and health and safety requirements thwarted plans to run it as a working heritage mill and museum.

☞ ☞ *You will need a car (or take a tour) to visit Parkside Limestone Quarry, near Weston. There are two routes. Follow Chelmer Street up past the public gardens, turn right at Parsons Road and follow it out to Airedale Road, to the quarry. Or take the main south road up Severn Street, follow Wansbeck Street past Awamoa Park, through Holmes Hill and turn right to take Weston Road out to Weston. Go north through Weston township along Airedale Road until you see the quarry gates.*

PARKSIDE LIMESTONE QUARRY
Airedale Road, ca. 2 km from Weston (not registered)

It is worth visiting the sole remaining limestone quarry. There used to be several. Quarrying began around Kakanui and Totara about 1862 and despite the shortcomings of the early anchorage, some of their output even found its way to Melbourne. Call it brand protection or monopoly capitalism, but over time the owners of the Weston quarry bought and closed the others, achieving a near monopoly by the 1920s. Gay's Quarry had cut its first loads in 1906, when J.H. Gay formed his company in conjunction with Parkside farmer Joseph R. Mitchell. Gay introduced power-driven circular sawing. Since the 1970s, the business has been known formally as Parkside Quarries, as the Mitchell family bought back in and renamed the business after their farm.

But this is all recent history. The story begins about 35 to 40 million years ago, when the sea stretched as far inland as Aviemore. Oamaru Stone (or Totara Limestone, to give it its correct geological name) originated in that shallow sea when the hard calcareous shells of marine mammals and plants fell to the sea floor. Over millions of years this sediment hardened, then was lifted above sea level. Oamaru Stone is mostly sand-sized bryozoan fragments and other microfossils but quarry staff sometimes find larger fossils of corals, molluscs, shark teeth or even penguin or whalebones. At Weston the limestone seam is about 40 metres thick and it contains enough stone to keep the saw blades busy for hundreds, if not thousands of years. You can watch people cutting out the two-tonne blocks with a huge electric double chainsaw mounted on rails and then follow its progress through the cutting shed, where it is split, sawn or bolstered. Every day, Parkside despatches about three house lots of stone veneer and also keeps the nearby limeworks busy. The precise rectangular sawmarks of the old flooded quarry face are the closest thing you will see to an Egyptian pyramid in the New Zealand. Take your sunglasses, though, because in summertime, the quarry floor can be blindingly white! See the Visitor Centre for directions or tour information.

Parkside Quarry
Forty million years ago a shallow sea covered North Otago. Now rail mounted mechanical saws cut it into blocks for dispatch to the quarry factory for cutting into house veneer.

Opposite: Visitors often compare the old quarry to the pyramids. As this view from the new quarry edge suggests, the limestone deposits go on for many, many kilometres.

Oamaru Events Calendar

Major, regular events only. For further information contact the Visitor Centre, www.tourism.waitaki.co.nz

January
Kurow Festival (begins Dec.)
Omarama Cup gliding championships

February
North Otago Dahlia Show
Whitestone Wine and Food Festival
North Otago Horticulture Society Summer Show

March
North Otago Organic Wine and Food Festival
Traditional Boats Day

April
Oamaru Offshore Fishing Classic

May
North Otago Horticultural Society Autumn Show

June
Midwinter Arts and Masks Festival

September/October
North Otago Horticultural Show

November
Victorian Heritage Celebrations
North Otago A & P Show (third Tuesday & Wednesday)

'Historic Port' heritage trail sign in Harbour Street.

FURTHER READING

Anderson, Atholl, *The Welcome of Strangers: the Ethnohistory of Southern Maori A.D. 1650–1850*, University of Otago Press, Dunedin, 1998

Brocklebank, Norris and Richard Greenaway, *Oamaru*, John McIndoe, Dunedin, 1979

Leaver-Cooper, Sheila and Ian S. Smith, *Janet Frame's Kingdom by the Sea: Oamaru*, Lincoln, Daphne Brasell Associates/Lincoln University Press, 1997

McCarthy, P. C., *Forrester and Lemon of Oamaru: Architects*, North Otago Branch Committee of the New Zealand Historic Places Trust, Oamaru, 2002

McDonald, K.C., *White Stone Country*, Oamaru, 1962

McLean, Gavin, *Oamaru Harbour: Port in a Storm*, Dunmore Press, Palmerston North, 1982

Shaw, Peter, *Whitestone Oamaru: a Victorian Architectural Heritage*, Craig Potton Publishing, Nelson, 1995

Wilson, John (ed.), *Parallel 45: a Waitaki Celebration of Otago's 150th Anniversary*, North Otago Branch Committee of the New Zealand Historic Places Trust, Oamaru, 1997

As well as the books listed here, I consulted: K.C. McDonald, *A History of Waitaki Boys' High School 1883–1958*, Christchurch, 1958; Ian Milner, *Milner of Waitaki*, Dunedin, 1983; Vincent O'Sullivan (ed.), *Intersecting Lines: the Memoirs of Ian Milner*, Wellington, 1993; Anthony Scott, *A History of the Oamaru Courthouse 1883–1983*, Wellington, 1983; W.H. Scotter, *Run, Estate and Farm*, Dunedin, 1948; Jane Thomson (ed.), *Southern People: A Dictionary of Otago Southland Biography*, Dunedin, 1998; Peter I. Whitlock, *75th Anniversary of Lodge Oamaru No. 260 1924–1990*, Oamaru, 1990; *The Dictionary of New Zealand Biography*, Vols 1–3, Auckland, 1990–96, the Historic Places Trust magazine *New Zealand Historic Places* and conservation plans and research reports held at the Trust's Wellington library.